D0422639

"If you don't know where you are going,
any road will take you there."

"The major strategic challenges for firms encompass how to please customers, win orders, and simultaneously achieve financial objectives on an ongoing basis."

"If a business has an excellent
strategy and effective implementation,
it will likely be successful."

How to Plan and Execute Strategy

✓ 24 Steps to Implement Any Corporate Strategy Successfully

WALLACE STETTINIUS
D. ROBLEY WOOD, JR.
JACQUELINE L. DOYLE
JOHN L. COLLEY, JR.

MCGRAW-HILL

New York Chicago San Francisco Lisbon
London Madrid Mexico City Milan New Delhi
San Juan Seoul Singapore Sydney Toronto

1 2 3 4 5 6 7 8 9 0 DOC/DOC 0 9 8 7 6

ISBN-13: 978-0-07-148437-4
ISBN-10:   0-07-148437-X

This book is printed on acid-free paper.

McGraw-Hill books are available at special quantity discounts to use as premiums and sales promotions, or for use in corporate training programs. For more information, please write to the Director of Special Sales, McGraw-Hill Professional, Two Penn Plaza, New York, NY 10121-2298. Or contact your local bookstore.

Contents

How to Plan and Execute Strategy

☑ Planning and executing strategy

Every business leader would like to create a sound strategy and have it executed well. Accomplishing this, however, remains an elusive goal for most business organizations.

Devising and implementing new and innovative strategies to exploit opportunities in a competitive world is daunting. Clearly, no one strategy fits all companies.

As with most complex problems, the solution to planning and executing strategy lies in creating a practical, step-by-step methodology that breaks the problem into managcable components to be addressed in a logical sequence. The 24 steps in this handbook describe such a systematic process.

What exactly is strategy?

Virtually everyone in our society is touched by the strategic choices firms make about their products and services. These decisions affect the workers, customers, competitors, investors, and communities of today's businesses.

The word strategy comes from the Greek word *strategos*, which means "a general," and is derived from roots meaning "army" and "lead." Hence, a general is the leader of an army. In both the military and business, competition typically drives organizations to find ways to best their rivals through the effective use of their resources.

Strategy is often contrasted with tactics, another term with military origins. While strategy represents the big picture about "doing the right things," tactics are more about the details of "doing things right." Strategy sets the *direction* in which the organization will proceed while tactics determine *how* it will proceed.

The major strategic challenges for firms encompass how to please customers, win orders, and simultaneously achieve financial objectives on an ongoing basis.

For example, a firm could have a strategy to build market share by selling the lowest-priced product in its market. After implementation of the strategy, the competitors will react, and the firm's strategy will need to adapt to meet the new challenges. There is no stopping point and no final battle. The competitive cycle continues on perpetually.

An organization's strategy should evolve over time as a blend of the intended strategy and the firm's responses to events, learning from experiences, and the emergence of new information and ideas. It is an iterative crafting process of making and implementing decisions, observing, analyzing, and learning from the results, and then making decisions anew.

To create, plan, and implement strategies, one should first learn to think in a way that combines the rational and the intuitive in analyzing both hard and soft data to arrive at a unique interpretation of opportunities.

The 24 steps contained in this book will guide you through the process of formulating and implementing strategy. Regardless of their content and brilliance, though, strategies will not be successful unless they are implemented effectively and updated regularly.

"Strategy is a process, not an event."

☐ ~~Skip the strategy~~

☑ **Manage strategically**

Many managers have a disdain for strategy and strategic planning, assuming that they are too theoretical for practical use. Every successful company, however, benefits from an effective strategy. The strategy might have been developed through formal analysis, trial and error, intuition, or just luck. Regardless of its origin, a strategy was indeed executed, whether managers were aware of it or not.

If a business has an excellent strategy and effective implementation, it will likely be successful. If a company has a poor strategy, however, it is probably going to fail in the long run. But what if a firm has a strength in strategy formulation *or* its ability to implement, but not both?

We know that some businesses have exceptional strategies and succeed in spite of mediocre operations. For others, it doesn't matter how well they make or deliver their product because nobody wants it. Great implementation simply cannot compensate for a poor strategy. Having an effective strategy, though, is not necessarily more important than effective implementation. In the end, we must acknowledge that a company needs both to guarantee success.

Strategy is a long-term concept and, importantly, deals with change. The leader of a business, in seeking a prosperous future, must consider what might lie ahead and understand the driving forces of change and their likely impact on the business. Managers must determine which actions they should be taking now to prepare for what they expect in and desire for the future.

Tactics, in contrast, focus on the present. Tactics emphasize taking actions to execute the strategy, such as meeting demand, satisfying customer needs and desires, improving efficiency, and controlling quality and costs so as to make a profit and meet other short-term goals.

Evidence that a business's current strategies and operations have been effective includes current profitability and positive trends. Management must continually question whether these current strategies will continue to be successful in the future. Although some strategies last a long time, successful strategies do not last forever. Environments evolve, competition intensifies, and requirements for leadership talent shift. Strategies must transform in response.

To benefit from using the strategic management process to develop and implement strategies:

Use it to provide a framework: You can use the process to face and prepare for the future. This also requires attention to the present and the short-term horizon.

Let it guide you logically while requiring creativity: The process requires the team to generate ideas as well as consider the administrative details and functional activities that must be coordinated for successful strategy implementation.

Ensure widespread participation, which culminates in decisive plans: As a result, the process improves communication, motivation, and execution.

"Every activity should begin with a vision, purpose, goals, and objectives. These dreams are not likely to be realized without an effective strategy."

☐ Just follow the steps

☑ Follow the logic

The strategic management process helps you first to understand your business's current situation and trends, next to determine a direction and desired state for the business, and finally to understand and identify what must be done to close the gap between the organization's current and desired positions.

Strategic management encompasses four tasks, each building on those that precede it:

- **Strategic learning** requires understanding the firm's operations and results. Learning also requires that you continually scan the environment and process the relevant information. The goal is to acquire a profound knowledge of the business and the environment in which it operates.

- **Strategic thinking** is a creative and analytical activity that builds on the knowledge developed in the learning phase. Through the strategic thinking phase, you determine *what you want to do* in a strategic sense and the issues that must be addressed for success.

■ **Strategic planning** has the aim of determining how best to *address strategic issues to achieve your strategic objectives*.

■ **Strategic action** involves the *implementation* and *execution* of the strategic plans. Strategic action should involve activity at all levels of the organization.

A diligent completion of the tasks and a willingness to learn—to see things in new ways—are prerequisites for an effective strategic management process.

Strategic thinking requires creativity, which generates wide ranges of options to be considered. The more options you develop, the more likely you are to find the best one. Strategic thinking also encompasses a series of strategic choices that should be guided by the vision, mission, and values of the organization, including the following:

■ What business do you want to be in?
■ In what direction do you want to take the business?
■ What are the goals of the business?
■ How are you going to compete?

■ What functional strategies do you need to be successful?

The functional strategies involve creating competencies throughout the organization to support the business strategy. The functions are generally considered to include marketing, production/operations, human resources, and finance. Detailed plans should be developed for various levels of the organization, all consistent with the articulated strategy.

Finally, the action phase of strategic management involves implementing the strategic plans. All members of the organization are involved in this phase of activity every day, whether mindful of it or not.

As you develop your strategic management skills:

Keep in mind that the strategic management process is deceptively simple: Learn, think, plan, and do. The devil is in the implementation.

Develop a profound knowledge of your business and its environment: These initial steps of the strategic management process build a foundation for the subsequent ones.

Assess constantly throughout the strategic management process: Continually review your implementation choices for consistency and fit.

"Continuous improvement is a requisite of competitiveness. Never let it rest.

☐ ~~Assume you~~ are ready

☑ Assess your readiness

Is your business ready to take on the challenge of creating, planning, and implementing a strategy? You can determine your readiness by answering several questions. Think of this as a *readiness audit*.

Why are you thinking about strategy at this time? Is it for the right reasons?

Are you considering your strategy because, while moderately successful, you have a gnawing discomfort that things might be beginning to deteriorate? Or, do you aspire to move your business to the next level of size, profitability, or performance? Are you facing unprecedented competition?

Does your business have the right leaders?

Leadership plays a major role in both creating and executing strategy. In fact, organizations seldom advance beyond the capability of their leaders. It is important to determine whether leaders throughout the organization are able and willing to commit to strategic management—especially those at the top.

The major distinction between day-to-day management and strategic leadership involves *perspective*.

Management focuses on the present, with emphasis on executing current strategies and meeting current performance objectives.

Strategic leadership focuses on the future, with emphasis on understanding the factors influencing the future, anticipating their likely impact on the business, setting longer-term goals, and developing strategies for achieving them.

Be certain your team has leadership capabilities for both activities.

Do you have a set of relevant guiding principles in place?

An organization should have a vision, a mission, and a set of core values that are relevant to its current situation and embraced by its leaders. The strategy and plans will be built upon these principles.

Are the right people in the right jobs?

The leader must get the right people in the right jobs and get rid of the wrong people. The right people solve problems and get things done without burdening management. The wrong people not only don't solve problems but also create additional problems and distractions.

Do any other current issues need to be addressed?

If a business has substantial internal or operational problems, lacks a viable business model, or is not adequately capitalized, the managers should address these issues before taking on strategic management.

Do the key managers understand the need to think more strategically? Are they personally committed to making the effort?

Understanding and commitment are necessary for success. Honest and realistic answers to the questions above will reveal whether your organization is ready to proceed.

To conduct your readiness audit, do the following:

Start by identifying the key leaders in the organization: Assess their willingness and capabilities to participate in a strategic management process.

Ensure that you have a relevant set of guiding principles: They will be the foundation of all strategic decisions going forward.

Identify any current issues, including personnel, that must be resolved: Attend to them before attempting any meaningful strategy work.

"You can only prep for so long; eventually you have to play the game."

☐ ~~Jump right in~~

☑ **Plan to plan**

Yore now ready to begin the strategic planning process. It is important to find a logical starting point for the work, one that recognizes efforts that are already under way and issues that have already been resolved.

A key decision is the level of the effort to which your management team will commit. Not all situations require the same level of effort, nor are all teams capable of undertaking an extensive effort. Three levels of effort—*abbreviated*, *moderate*, and *extensive*—are described below.

In an *abbreviated* process, the CEO and other key executives typically carry out the strategic planning work, with the help of perhaps a few others, carefully selected. The process is essentially a series of meetings, with research and analytical tasks done by individuals or small teams. The outcomes should include a competitive strategy for the organization, functional strategies, and action plans for critical issues and initiatives.

In a *moderate* process, the effort is expanded to include a few task forces, especially for conducting research and analyzing results. The task forces will include members from the functional areas likely to be affected by the strategic process. The outcomes of a moderate process should include those for the abbreviated process plus more thorough integration of the strategic goals into operating goals, budgets, and plans.

In an *extensive* process, the CEO often delegates the work to a steering committee, with a champion as chair. The champion should be a person who is respected throughout the organization, knows the business well, can think conceptually, has good people skills, and is well organized. Enthusiasm for the effort is important. The champion should report directly to the CEO for the process.

The steering committee under the champion should have a cross-functional and multi-layered membership. In particular, the steering committee should establish the task forces and monitor their efforts to gather and analyze information and make recommendations. The steering committee should also develop a master work plan that delineates the schedules, responsibilities, and deliverables. Outcomes should mirror those for the moderate process with a totally integrated planning cycle.

Regardless of the complexity of your situation, the following three directions will help you start planning your approach to strategic management:

Select a logical starting point: It should build on what has previously been decided, as well as the company's agreed-upon current competitive position. Make sure all key objectives, goals, and assumptions are clear to all participants.

Determine the level of the effort required: The effort typically reflects the complexity of the situation. The process should be the simplest and least cumbersome for the circumstances.

Design an appropriate process: Outline plans to perform the work in a logical sequence. Avoid building elaborate systems that generate ponderous written documents and wear out the participants.

"Designing a process to fit the circumstances in a given situation is the foundation for a successful implementation of strategic management."

☑ Define your businesses

To plan and implement strategy, you must first determine if you are in more than one business. Defining business segments is a cornerstone of the strategic management process. A company must develop, nurture, and implement basic strategies for each business in which it engages.

If your organization is a holding company with numerous business units, it is obvious that it has multiple businesses. A business unit or division is typically a semi-autonomous or autonomous organization consisting of at least one independent business and possibly more. Holding company strategies address the appropriateness of the various business units (and potential acquisition targets) for inclusion in the corporate portfolio.

Segmenting your firm's activities into its distinct businesses will be complicated, however, when lines of business are integrated and share strategies or resources.

The following questions will help you identify which businesses are strategically separable:

■ Does the unit have a clear set of external customers? Are the majority of sales made outside the firm? An internal supplier may be an operating unit but not necessarily an independent business.

■ Does the unit have a group of external competitors?

■ Does management of this unit have discretion over the nature of products and services offered, and the authority to develop the recommended course of action regarding products and markets?

■ Does management of this unit have the authority to make crucial operating decisions, such as choosing suppliers and distribution channels?

■ Is it possible to measure the financial performance of this unit? A business unit must be a true profit center; its revenues and/or expenses (and hence profits) must not be the result of negotiations among organizations within the firm.

Operating units that do not satisfy most of the above criteria will probably have problems managing their own affairs and most often do not qualify as true businesses.

Consider the following three concepts when identifying a firm's businesses:

Apply the strategic management process at both the corporate and the business unit levels: At the corporate or holding company level, the task is one of portfolio management. What businesses do you want to be in or exit? How will you allocate resources? At the business level, competitive strategies are developed and implemented.

Recognize that business segmentation is key in the development of a strategic management process: It is at the business unit level that the most time and effort are required and where strategies that address issues such as product offerings and attributes, marketing decisions, and pricing are developed.

Prepare to address organizational structure often as you change your strategies: The structure of the organization must support your strategies. Do not ignore, however, the benefits to the organization of shared services and economies of scale and scope when making organizational adjustments.

"Strategies are formulated at the level of the business. Before you formulate strategies, you must first determine how many businesses you have."

☐ Assume you are informed

☑ Assess your situation

The purpose of this step is to ensure that you have a realistic knowledge of your business as it is operating currently.

The status of a business can be described in terms of both *condition* (strength or weakness) and *momentum* or *trends* (improving, stable, or declining). A strong business condition implies that *past* strategies have worked well. A positive momentum suggests that *current* strategies are effective.

One commonly used tool, the SWOT analysis, assesses the firm's internal *strengths* and *weaknesses* and the *opportunities* and *threats* presented by the external environment. The underlying assumption of this analysis is that you can formulate new strategies more effectively after you have carefully reviewed the related characteristics of the organization.

The analysis can range from a few executives brainstorming to rigorous research. Some firms seek feedback from their customers to gain insight into their perceptions of the firm's strengths and weaknesses. Peer-company benchmarks should be used wherever possible to provide a careful review of the business's financial performance.

You might also choose to use activity or value chain analysis for analyzing your current situation. The value chain of a business identifies the various activities involved in creating and delivering value to the customer.

In evaluating your current situation, you might find it helpful to think in terms of competencies and competitive advantage.

- A *competency* is an internal activity that you perform well, often better than other internal activities.
- A *core* competency is a well-performed internal activity that is central to your strategy, competitiveness, and profitability. Core competencies are the critical success factors that link internal activities to the customers' needs.
- A *distinctive* competency is a competitively valuable activity that you perform better than your rivals. Distinctive competencies are those that provide a competitive advantage.

Competencies form the foundation of strategies that become difficult for your competitors to duplicate.

Finally, you should determine how your firm wins orders in the marketplace. The purpose of the assessment is to identify the value-adding activities your firm is able to do better than your competitors. You should subsequently consider the sustainability of these advantages—how difficult it would be for a competitor to reach your level of performance.

Here are three tips for conducting an assessment of your current situation:

Don't overanalyze your current situation: You can't possibly examine everything that conceivably could have an impact on your performance. Focus on what is important first.

Think SWOT: The matching of opportunities and threats in the external environment with the firm's internal strengths and weaknesses provides the foundation for developing competitive strategies.

Identify differences: In any industry, firms will differ in how well they perform various activities. These performance differences create opportunities for firms that have a clear knowledge of their business.

"Successful companies confront the facts of their situations."

☐ Don't bother with details

☑ Understand your model

A thorough understanding of your firm's business model is necessary for formulating and implementing strategy. The business model of an organization encompasses the realities that determine the profitability of the firm: volume and revenue, costs and profitability, and capitalization.

Volume is the driving force of a business model. Sales volume translates internally into the resources needed to deliver the expected amount of goods and services in a timely fashion.

Revenue is the result of volume and prices. Pricing strategies are generally among the most important decisions management makes, because they not only determine unit revenue but also impact the number of units sold and, hence, total revenue. Pricing is a crucial strategic decision.

Businesses have different economic characteristics determined by their expense structures. An understanding of the cost structure of your business, particularly the distribution of fixed and variable costs, is essential. In general, businesses with high fixed costs must place special emphasis on achieving volume sales goals; those with low fixed costs should focus on price.

Businesses have different economic structures in terms of investment intensity, i.e., the quantity of assets required to support a dollar of sales. Process manufacturing businesses, such as paper mills or power generating stations, are very asset-intensive. Service businesses in general are less capital-intensive.

Determine what drives profitability. Which products are most important in generating profits? Which customers? How do you win these orders? How do you (or your competitors) create loyal customers? Which drives your profitability—volume or pricing?

Consider the Return on Investment (ROI), i.e., the relationship between profits and the investment required to generate them. The financial marketplace sets the desired ROI based on perceived risk. Examine benchmarks for appropriate measures of ROI, such as return on equity, return on net assets, and return on assets.

The final part of the business model is the decision on *how to fund the required investment.*

Short-term borrowing can be used for temporary asset requirements such as seasonal inventories. Long-term requirements such as fixed assets should be funded by long-term capital—either debt or equity. Internally generated funding is also a very attractive source of funds. Does your business model generate free cash flow?

Below are three tips for understanding your business model:

Do the analysis: Gather the data, take the time, and solicit the range of perspectives needed to guarantee a sound understanding of the business model.

Identify the key drivers of profitability: Examine products, customers, and fixed and variable costs. Do not overlook the relationships among your products; loss leaders might create opportunities for truly profitable accompanying sales.

Do not overlook funding and investment requirements: Owners, shareholders, and parent corporations expect a fair return on their investment. Inability to provide this return indicates a deficiency in the business model.

"The interfaces between marketing, manufacturing, and finance must provide for a profitable operation."

☐ ~~Know your products~~

✓ Know your market

One of the important challenges of strategy formulation and implementation is to thoroughly understand the markets you serve and the needs and desires of your customers. This understanding will be essential in developing your marketing strategy, which must match market preferences with existing and potential products or services.

Numerous *social and political factors* affect the attractiveness of the environment in which a business functions, including demographics and trends, laws and regulations, taxation and subsidies, power of special interest groups, unionization, and societal attitudes. The strategist must identify and take advantage of these macro trends.

Some industries are more attractive than others because of the *competitive dynamics of the players*. Michael Porter of the Harvard Business School has identified five forces that define industry competition:

The threat of new entrants
The power of buyers
The power of suppliers
The threat of substitutes
The intensity of rivalry among existing competitors

Each of these forces asserts an influence on industry competitiveness and profitability.

The *market* in which a business operates may have characteristics that are somewhat different from the industry in general. The market is usually defined by some combination of type of customer, product or service, and/or geography. Important factors you will want to understand are:

Market maturity, cyclicality, and/or seasonality
Market size (dollars and units) and growth rate, by segment
Market share distribution among competitors
Market sensitivity to product offerings and price changes
Switching costs of customers
Pricing power

Financial characteristics are also an essential consideration when deciding on entering, remaining in, or leaving a business. Financial characteristics include profitability and margin structure, capital intensity, capacity utilization, and financial barriers to entry and exit.

Consider these three things when conducting your analyses and developing responses:

Don't fight the macro trends or industry forces: Instead, identify them and hitch a ride. Pursue strategies that position your company so it can take advantage of trends, best defend itself against industry forces, or influence the trends or forces in its favor.

Look for a growing market: Finding an attractive market that is growing and in which you have the skills and resources to compete will pay off in many ways. A growing market will allow firms to grow even while they lose market share, providing an opportunity for other firms to grow aggressively and capture share.

Critically assess the needs and desires of your customers—and potential customers: Assign creative and open people to this essential task and make sure it gets the attention it deserves. A cornerstone of strategy formulation is determining what customers really want and need—not just what you think they want and need.

"The business graveyard is full of firms that failed to understand their markets."

☐ ~~Trust in the~~ status quo

☑ Assess the terrain

Before devising strategies, you must understand the competitive landscape as it exists and as it is changing. You should examine and understand what competitors have done in the past, are doing now, and are likely to do in the future. The aim of this assessment is to find, for your firm going forward, a unique and defensible mix of product, marketing, and pricing strategies, given the direction your competitors will likely take.

This approach requires a thorough understanding of competitors' strengths and weaknesses, leadership, resources, and goals in order to estimate their possible approaches to competition. It is also useful to examine a benchmarking analysis comparing your organization's financial results with those of your competitors.

You must also examine forces driving change, which are related to but different from industry competitive forces. Driving forces create the opportunity for significant change at a particular point in time. An example of a driving force is the impact of the Internet on service firms.

While the environment is complex, most significant change is driven by only a few driving forces. You need to begin by identifying the primary forces and then understand their trends and potential impact on your industry, customers, and business.

Important activities involved in understanding driving forces of change include:

- *Identification*—Survey your firm's environment to detect changes already under way that might impact your business. Pay particular attention to technology, regulations, and the links in your supply chain.
- *Monitoring*—Once you've identified the driving forces, monitor them systematically.
- *Competitive intelligence*—Understand your rivals' strengths and weaknesses as well as how they might influence changes in the industry's competitive structure and, in particular, your relative position.

Remember: you are not really trying to predict the future, but to better understand possibilities and probabilities so that you can take an appropriate stance as you make your strategic decisions. An important caution is to recognize the degree of uncertainty inherent in your situation and judiciously make accommodations for it.

Here are three tips to keep in mind as you search for competitive advantages and relevant driving forces:

Know your industry: If you don't get the facts, the facts will get you. Do not overestimate or underestimate your competitors; you cannot know them too well.

You can't exploit a force you don't understand or a trend you haven't identified: You are looking for relevant forces that are not under the control of your firm or industry but that can profoundly change the way business is conducted. Be vigilant.

Incorporate the driving forces into your strategies: Go forward; get started down the learning curve. If you don't, a competitor will.

"If you don't get the facts, the facts will get you."

☑ Understand opportunities and threats

The purpose of most strategy implementation efforts is to exploit opportunities and/or to counter threats. You have the advantage of being able to select the opportunities to pursue. Threats, on the other hand, may be imposed on you.

Where should we look to identify opportunities and threats? Major sources include the industry (for substitute products or disruptive technologies), competitors (to assess their strengths and weaknesses), the general environment (for economic, social, political, or technological events and trends), and the organization's specific environment (for shifts in market characteristics). In particular, listen to your customers' feedback and questions.

It is usually better for your firm to be the first to acknowledge and exploit applicable new developments. A head start gives you the first-mover advantages of experience, scale, and recognition over later entrants. On the other hand, advantages sometimes accrue to followers, who learn through observation and typically invest far less than leaders.

You should *devise ways of exploiting identified opportunities*. What resources and competencies will be required? Are they available? If not, how might you get them? Is there a limited time window for the opportunity? What are the attendant risks? How do you minimize them? Are they risks that you can afford to take? Can you risk **not** acting?

You should also *consider creating additional opportunities through stretch objectives or breakthrough strategies*, by which you think the unthinkable and then work to bring about the desired results. Consider, for example, what it would take to ensure that you win all of your bids or capture all of the business of your largest customers. How can you get there or at least move in that direction?

Threats are external conditions in the firm's environment that carry potentially negative consequences. Examples of threats are changes in customers' needs or tastes, substitute products, inadequate supplies of skilled labor or raw materials, new government regulations, and potential litigation.

Threats must be evaluated continually. How likely are they to materialize? How soon? What is their potential impact if they do materialize? How can you reduce it? For which ones should you prepare immediately?

Here are three tips for managing your opportunities and threats:

Identify and exploit opportunities: That's the essence of success. Give widespread recognition to employees who find ways to innovate. Place bets on multiple new products and services; some will pay off handsomely, but be prepared to lose your total investment on products that fail.

Do not ignore threats: That attitude could lead to failure. Be attentive to identifying and monitoring potential threats to your business. A failure to do so could mean devastating results.

Take time to think the unthinkable about your company and its products: This exercise will stretch your thinking and help you uncover valuable opportunities.

"You cannot know too much about your customers or your competitors."

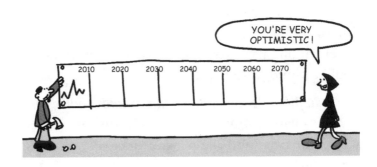

☐ Accept whatever results

☑ Set feasible goals

For nearly every business, the most important measures of corporate performance are the interrelated goals of return on investment (ROI); growth in revenues, earnings, or market share; and adequacy of cash flow to fund the growth.

The appropriateness of a company's goals can be measured by comparisons with the performance of companies in the same industry and, ultimately, the wider array of investment opportunities across the spectrum of all industries, as firms compete for investment capital.

In the matter of corporate goals and performance, it is essential that you choose a business in which to compete that offers a reasonable chance of meeting your financial goals and objectives.

The first element of strategy formulation is to select the business in which you will compete. If it is determined that entering into or continuing in an industry is likely to be successful, the strategist must determine the direction the business will take (strategy) and the force (level of investment) that will be devoted to the effort.

There are essentially three directional growth paths from which you must choose: growth, stability/maturity, and retrenchment. Each path corresponds with a major phase of every industry's product life cycle and each has different financial demands and rewards.

Here are some questions that may help you identify the various stages of the industry/product life cycle:

In the business under consideration, is the number of competitors increasing or decreasing? The number of competitors typically increases during the growth stage and decreases during retrenchment.

Do you expect to have pricing power? Price increases are often easier during growth and almost impossible during maturity and retrenchment.

Entry also becomes more difficult as established firms build barriers in the late growth and maturity stages.

Fast-growing product lines are typically profitable, but have high investment requirements. As the products and markets mature, profits continue, investment requirements diminish, and the business generates cash.

During retrenchment, profits fall, the business continues to generate cash but at a reduced rate, and additional investment becomes less and less attractive. At some point, you will need to harvest the business to recover as much of the invested capital as possible by withholding or reducing investment, liquidation, or divestment.

Here are three things to remember when setting goals and objectives and using the industry/product life cycle to improve strategic decisions:

Start by setting feasible goals: Goals must be appropriate for the return potential of the chosen business. If they are not, one or the other must change.

Be aware of industry characteristics: Before implementing a new strategy, consider what makes sense for the business, given the stage of the industry/product life cycle. This consideration will help you choose the appropriate directional growth path for your business.

Aim high: Organizations rarely exceed their expectations. Plan for breakthroughs and they will be more likely to occur.

"Competing in the wrong industry at the wrong time is inviting defeat."

☑ Strategize for goals

After selecting the business, setting goals, and determining the directional growth path, the next step is to develop strategies to achieve the desired objectives.

Competitive strategy is about acquiring and sustaining an advantage over competitors in the industry through performing differently in some meaningful way. Michael Porter, of the Harvard Business School, has identified three generic paths to achieving competitive advantage:

- *Overall cost leadership:* no competitor across the industry can offer an equivalent product or service at a lower cost.
- *Differentiation:* a company differentiates its offerings in some way that is meaningful to the customers.
- *Focus:* achieve low cost and/or differentiation for a narrow market, group of customers, or segment of the product line.

These three generic strategies are not necessarily mutually exclusive, but most firms find it difficult to pursue even one successfully.

Strategy sets the direction for the business: its goal should be to maintain or develop a sustainable advantage over competitors. In developing your strategy, consider the information gathered and analyses performed in the previous steps. You will need to articulate the attributes of your products or services, which should be aligned with the needs and/or the desires of the customers. The accompanying pricing strategy must be predicated on both costs and competition. Define the marketing strategy further by identifying geographic, market, distribution, and promotional strategy decisions.

The outcome should be the definition of a defensible competitive position—either different enough that competitors will not challenge it or built on an advantage that is sustainable.

Here are some examples: offering the lowest-priced product in a market (overall cost leadership); providing products or services that are best-in-class on a dimension valued by your customers (differentiation); and delivering a product or a service to a specific, limited customer group or market, such as one defined by geographic area, or concentrating on one part of the product line (focus or *niche*). A best-cost provider strategy combines low cost and differentiation to deliver value and achieve a unique competitive position.

The practical goal of a strategy is to provide customers with a product or service in a manner such that no competitor can deliver an equivalent or superior product or service at a lower cost in the markets chosen.

Here are three tips for crafting strategies:

Base your strategies on some source of competitive advantage: That's the key to success. Generic sources include low cost, differentiation, and focus.

Consider the relationship between competitive advantage and the industry life cycle: The skills needed to build competitive advantage change as generations of products move through the industry life cycle.

Don't ignore the importance of functional competencies and resources: You must align the functional strategies with the business strategies. Do not assume that functional competencies or resources are adequate to support a given strategy. Before launching a new strategy, assess your capabilities and needs.

"Strategy formulation gives you direction. Think of your travels as just beginning."

☑ Set priorities

S*trategic initiatives* are specific activities intended to address the big-picture issues and close the gap between the current state and the desired future state. They may be aimed at taking advantage of opportunities or solving problems.

Strategic initiatives are imperative when your firm faces a performance gap. Gaps appear when performance projections with current strategies are not likely to meet management and shareholder expectations. The gaps point to issues that call for adjusting current strategies, adopting new strategies, or both. Before creating initiatives, you must first identify and set priorities for the strategic issues that need to be addressed. Each major strategic issue may require one or more initiatives.

Strategic initiatives are often aimed at solving problems or making major strides toward implementing a new strategy. If you are addressing a shortcoming, try to determine if the problem can be turned into an opportunity. Sometimes merely solving a problem will not make a business successful. In many situations, success lies in identifying and exploiting opportunities through carefully crafted strategic initiatives.

To be effective, you should identify strategic issues, develop initiatives for each, and set priorities for the order of those initiatives. A business seldom has enough resources to take on all of its high-impact strategic issues at any given time.

To make these determinations, you must answer two contextual questions. How much time do you have to respond? A critical window of opportunity or looming deadline will create a sense of urgency that determines time frames. Is there a critical path? Strategic issues may have to be addressed in a certain sequence.

Even if you must persevere to find the required resources or if you must purchase expertise outside the firm, you must take positive action to effect the desired strategic change. Each strategic initiative may require a number of separate, supporting proposals. Simple initiatives may not require elaborate planning, but as issues become more complex, comprehensive action plans or even project management will be necessary.

Here are three suggestions for dealing with strategic issues and initiatives:

Do not assume that your firm has the capability of seizing an opportunity: No firm has the financial, technological, and human resources to benefit from every opportunity. Opportunism without capability is a recipe for failure.

Be alert to possible showstoppers: When dealing with strategic issues, order and tradeoffs do matter. If an offer to purchase your company arrives unexpectedly, for example, it's a strategic issue that immediately preempts all others.

Consider timing: Time pressures often limit the amount of information that can be gathered to analyze strategic issues. Unfortunately, waiting too long to react can be just as disastrous as moving too quickly.

"The most important issues must be attacked first."

☐ Just sum up the parts

☑ Pursue your purpose

The holding company strategic plan articulates the purpose of the business and sets its direction. It must be consistent with the previously discussed statements of mission, vision, and values that form the basis for all lower-level decision making. We review these briefly here.

The mission articulates the purpose of the organization. A holding company encompasses a portfolio of businesses. Its purpose or mission sets out the types of businesses in which it aims to engage and the interrelationships of the businesses. A portfolio can range from a group of businesses focused on a particular industry, production methodology, type of customer, or other commonality to a group of diversified companies with little in common and virtually no interaction.

The vision describes the long-term direction. A holding company evolves or changes primarily by making acquisitions and divestitures and through the changing performance of its holdings, so its vision may be described in terms of the number, size, and types of subsidiary companies it pursues, creates, or divests.

Values define traits of individual employees or the organization as a whole.

The holding company boundaries are established by policies. One major policy for a holding company is its degree of centralization, defining or limiting the activities to be conducted within the holding company and the activities to be conducted in the subsidiary businesses. Other policies may address the systems for allocating capital, pension plans, transfer prices, or market boundaries among business units.

The holding company must prepare a strategic plan. That plan begins with its goals and objectives, which invariably include expectations for the growth in revenues and earnings, cash flow, and the return on shareholder equity (ROE).

The strategic plan also should specify in some way the degree of diversification intended for the portfolio of businesses and the degree of centralization or decentralization of planning and control.

Finally, the plan should address the approaches for allocating resources. It is implicit that the allocation of cash available from the common primary sources of reserves, operations, divestitures, and debt provides deliberate direction for the firm's development.

Three things to remember when formulating and implementing holding company strategies are:

Develop and implement strategies appropriate to the level, mission, vision, and values: Most holding company strategies are unique to that level. Holding company strategies deal primarily with meeting portfolio management objectives and rarely address competitive business strategies.

Keep in mind the purpose of the company: Holding company executives may be bankers in disguise. Managing the corporate balance sheet and reallocating capital to take advantage of the best opportunities is a key job of holding company executives.

Be practical with resources: In the end, the holding company is an overhead expense. The holding company headcount should be kept very small relative to that of the rest of the firm. The corporate office does not produce revenue, but may create considerable expense.

"The diversified, decentralized company has replaced the conglomerate of earlier years."

☐ ~~Don't bother~~ with plans

☑ Follow your mission

Business units or subsidiaries of holding companies follow steps nearly identical to those taken by independent, focused businesses when developing strategies and strategic plans.

The strategic plan for a business unit or independent business is a high-level conceptual document that articulates the purpose of the business and sets its direction. It addresses creating and serving customers.

The mission statement of a business articulates its purpose and provides a guiding aim or intention. A business unit of a holding company may have its own mission statement, but all of its guiding principles should be consistent with those of the parent company.

The primary purpose of a business can be described in terms of whom it will serve, the types of products or services it will provide, and how, in general, it plans to meet the needs of the target customers. Strategic clarity about the purpose of the business is critical because the purpose delineates what the company does and does not do.

The strategy statement of a business unit or focused business should specifically address how the business will win orders and satisfy the needs of its customers. Business-level strategies address the positioning of the business within its industry and typically include, in some form, the chosen generic competitive strategy: cost leadership, differentiation, or focus.

A business unit's strategic plan delineates its long-term direction and objectives. Broad strategic objectives describe what the business aspires to achieve or become. Those objectives should reflect the realities of the industry situation and the financial and human resources required to compete successfully. As with the corporate parent, financial goals should address growth, cash flow, and return on investment.

A strategic plan should include a definition of the skills or competencies that are critical to meeting the needs of customers and executing the strategy. Supporting functional strategies are intended to provide the requisite competencies necessary to implement chosen competitive strategies.

Strategic plans should describe important actions (tactics) to achieve the goals and objectives and to identify and set priorities for the actions that must be taken to implement the strategies.

The strategic plan should also provide detail for the short-term (one year) projections of growth, strategic moves, and supporting tactics, along with management's best thoughts as to likely plans and developments over the next three to five years.

Three tips for formulating and implementing business level strategies are:

Think about winning orders in the marketplace: Consider why customers should and will choose your products over competing products.

Remember your position in the industry: Everything you do is within the context of the industry situation and relative to what your competitors are doing.

Use the strategic plan document as a communications piece: Communications play a key role in implementing strategy, and the strategic plan should be used for this purpose in your business.

"A focused business needs a strategic plan to communicate its objectives and strategies."

☐ Trust your instinct
and luck

☑ Write the business plan

You might need an effective business plan to obtain approval and funding for your strategies or it might simply be a tool to move you toward implementation. Regardless, the business plan should start with an executive summary of its thrusts and emphasize products, services, growth, and anticipated levels of return on investment, rather than detailed financial analyses.

Use a planning horizon for your business plan that is long enough to provide the lead times necessary to obtain the required resources, yet short enough to be realistic. The planning horizon might typically include a three-year period, with quarterly projections for the first 12-month period and annual projections for the remaining two years. Under the scheme described, business plans should be updated quarterly or when new initiatives require.

One of the goals of the business plan is to develop a business model that reasonably reflects the relationships among volume, price, cost, and capacity. The first step in this process is to estimate revenues using projections of unit sales of products or services and assumptions about pricing levels. The second step involves projecting the expenses associated with the projected volumes, examining both variable costs and fixed costs. These elements combined create a high-level profit and loss statement prior to debt service.

You should also project a high-level balance sheet in order to estimate the resources required to operate at the projected scale. You will need to prepare a projection of the working capital and fixed assets (property, buildings, and equipment) required to support projected operations, as well as projected levels of long-term debt or equity.

Now you may project the interest costs and principal repayments for the horizon, taking into account any funding of new assets with additional debt in the planned capital structure.

Finally, you should supplement the income statement and balance sheet projections with a projected cash flow statement. *The projections will provide you with the information necessary to determine whether you will meet your goals for growth, cash flow, and return on investment.* Use this information to determine whether adjustments must be made and plans reworked.

Three things to remember when preparing a business plan are:

Summarize clearly and cogently: The summary at the beginning of the business plan may be the only part of your strategy documentation that others will read. It must be direct and crystal clear. The best strategies are meaningless if not approved and funded.

Be realistic in your projections: Strategic financial projections for more than one year—and almost certainly beyond three—are often acts of imagination. Accuracy diminishes rapidly as horizons extend.

Keep in mind that cash is king: For many organizations, the standard for determining the economic value of an investment is a discounted cash flow analysis. Furthermore, without cash, a business will grind to a halt.

"A business plan quantifies the scale and scope of your objectives on a time line."

☐ ~~Don't plan your~~ actions

☑ **Write the annual plan**

Congratulations! It is time to make things happen. The annual plan or budget is one of the basic vehicles through which strategies are executed. Every firm should produce an annual plan for the next calendar or fiscal year that documents the required resources in extreme detail, as well as the cost of implementing the new strategic initiatives.

The annual plan includes strategic, operating, and financial expectations for the coming year and is concerned with the coordination and control of internal flows of resources. It is the next step in refining the strategic plan and the business plan. The elements of an annual plan are:

- The action plans for the initiatives intended to achieve strategic goals
- A marketing/sales plan that projects volume sufficient to meet sales goals

- A volume/capacity plan that reconciles projected volumes with available capacity (plant, equipment, and labor)
- A capital budget that appropriates the funding for required equipment and other fixed assets
- An expense budget that projects the costs of the forecast volumes
- Financial statements (income statement, balance sheet, and cash flow statement) that establish financial expectations

These results will be compared with the goals of the parent company and/or the business unit.

Effective annual plans are integrated into the strategic management processes of the business. These processes include assessing the competitive environment and the firm's strengths and weaknesses and identifying the actions required to position the company. These management processes link the annual plan to the business plan and the strategic plan. A proposed, regular calendar for developing these plans follows:

- The first quarter is spent gathering information and assessing the situation.
- Second-quarter efforts include identifying issues, formulating strategies, and writing the strategic plan.
- The third quarter is the time to refine the strategic plan and develop the business plan, placing

special emphasis on the capital plan, which addresses the investment base of the business.

■ The fourth quarter is the time to write the annual plan for the coming year.

Here are three things to remember when building your annual plan:

Let the budget be a result of the planning process: If you start with a budget, it will act as a constraint on strategic planning. Let the benefits of implementing the strategic plans justify the budget.

Put control and accountability into the annual plan: Each strategic initiative should have a specific timeframe for completion. Include financial and operational milestones so management can monitor the implementation progress.

Involve all levels of management in your annual planning cycle: Managers at the corporate, business, and functional levels must reach agreement on various aspects of strategic initiatives as they move through the annual planning process. Choices should be made with an eye to corporate or business objectives and market realities.

"An annual plan specifies the actions required to implement your strategies one year at a time."

☐ Trust the strategies
to work

☑ Get the right people

The skills and abilities of employees are essential to successful strategy implementation. The goal is very simple: get the right people in the right jobs and get rid of the wrong people. Jim Collins's book *Good to Great* expresses this imperative as "getting the right people on the bus" and into "the right seats."

An important first requirement for finding the right people is the ability to judge people—their talent, character, and potential. Many companies employ formal testing, extensive group interview processes, and thorough reference checks to help with this process. A good rule is "When in doubt, do not hire." Hiring mistakes are very often difficult and costly to correct.

Who are the right people? They share the firm's values and they are competent. They have the skills and experience to do their jobs. They function independently and take responsibility. They are team players who interact appropriately and take pride in their accomplishments.

To improve the results of your organization and enhance the success of strategy implementation efforts, you must be willing and able to deal with people who are not performing well enough or who do not share the organization's values. Your employee evaluation system, therefore, must consider the dual dimensions of competence and values.

Employees who fit on both dimensions are obviously valuable resources, while it is equally clear that you must separate those who fit on neither attribute. Those who share the firm's values but lack competencies may be trainable, but those who do not share the firm's values should be let go, regardless of their competencies. Most often, this latter action brings relief to your loyal employees and deepens their trust in your commitment to a productive workplace.

Finally, once you have found the right people, provide continued education, training, and development. Continually work to put them in the best position to use their talents.

The following are three things to remember when selecting those who will implement your strategy:

Emphasize execution skills: That's essential. Put your faith in people, not just new products or services. Good people will find ways to implement their assigned strategic initiatives or understand why they cannot be implemented.

Align the competencies of key people with the strategy: Implementing different strategies requires different skills sets. For a differentiation strategy, find a person with industry knowledge, marketing skills, and the ability to motivate people and promote creativity. For a low-cost strategy, recruit a person with skills in devising lean operations, implementing tight financial controls, and relentlessly seeking continuous improvement.

Hire for attitude; educate for skill: The key is to hire people with the right values, attitudes, and social skills that lead to success in almost all jobs. Employees can learn how to operate technology, but it is difficult to teach people to be pleasant.

"Even the ideal strategy is useless unless properly implemented. Getting the right people is the cornerstone of executing strategy."

☐ ~~Let buy-in be optional~~

☑ **Obtain commitment**

Successful implementation hinges on widespread understanding of the strategy. As a result, you must ensure that your strategy is clearly communicated to all employees. This communication must not be a one-time, front-end exercise; it must be an ongoing activity that is an essential component of your implementation effort.

When strategies propose major changes, leaders must be prepared for resistance. People resist change for a variety of reasons, some rational and some emotional. Often, comfort with the status quo causes many people to feel threatened by any substantial change. For some, though, resistance might be rooted in the realization that they may not benefit personally from the proposed changes.

Your communication of the strategic plans must explain their aims and initiatives, why they are necessary, and what impact they will have on the organization. When there are conflicts of interest or the potential for some people involved to be hurt by the proposed changes, you should be straightforward. A leader should be trustworthy and demonstrate concern for all employees.

Commitment to the strategy is essential at all levels and must begin at the top. After achieving buy-in from senior executives, the strategic planning team should systematically roll out the message to everybody else throughout the organization. The members of the leadership team should be highly visible and demonstrate their commitment, individually and collectively, with consistent messages delivered in a variety of settings. The top managers should communicate to the middle managers and the middle managers should communicate to their staffs. Everyone should be included.

The most compelling way to communicate is in person and to groups small enough to permit interaction. Large group presentations can also be effective, particularly if they are supported by subsequent small group meetings. Some companies are enamored with expansive events. These occasions can be very symbolic and build enthusiasm, but they cannot be a substitute for substantive and interactive small group meetings.

Here are three things to keep in mind when planning to communicate strategies and foster commitment to making them succeed:

Involve people in your initiatives: That is the key to communication and commitment. Sustained involvement will foster cooperation, commitment, and enthusiasm. Involve employees at all levels in rolling out the strategy. The regular communication of progress in implementation will support and promote mutual commitment

Communicate to achieve understanding: People can't implement what they don't understand. Understanding gives purpose and meaning to a person's work. Misunderstanding creates confusion and distrust. The goal is to communicate so clearly that you gain extraordinary commitment.

Bear in mind that opposition will happen: A new strategic initiative that alters long-standing routines and personal relationships will be resisted. Use communication to build an awareness of the need for change. Use informal meetings to neutralize rumors and speculation.

"People can't implement what they don't understand."

☐ Fit strategies to status quo

☑ Align with strategy

You have been getting the right people in place and communicating your plans to gain understanding and support. You must also take time to deliberately align your structure, systems, and culture with your strategy. Success is unlikely without this effort.

Begin with the organizational structure. Structures are typically depicted by organization charts that show managerial positions, lines of authority, and reporting responsibilities. Traditional structures are hierarchical, with a series of layers, and most use some variation of a functional organizational structure to increase efficiency by standardizing practices, allowing people to specialize, and centralizing decision making. As businesses grow, they may develop other organizing themes, such as products, markets, or geography.

Ensure that the structure matches the central aims of the strategy. It should allow for reasonable resolution of conflicts as well as implementation of strong internal controls to set policies and goals, report results, and inform top managers. Delegation without effective controls amounts to abdication.

You should also align the organization's systems with the strategy. Make sure each system is structured to support the goals and objectives of your strategy. Key systems include:

- Communication systems
- Management information systems
- Planning and budgeting systems
- Human resources management systems

Pay special attention to the human resources systems, given the strategic importance of employees. Major elements of human resources management systems include:

- Recruiting and placement
- Development and training
- Performance measurement and evaluation
- Compensation, with special emphasis on incentives

Finally, you will want to align the culture with the new strategic plans. Positive cultures that value performance and focus on satisfying the customer will contribute to the success of the new strategic initiatives. Cultures that are divisive and focus on protecting the status quo or the interests of managers or employees will hinder the success of the new strategies.

The culture should embrace important attributes essential to implementing the strategy successfully. For example, a differentiation strategy emphasizing customer service should be supported by a culture valuing helpfulness and responsiveness to customer needs.

The following are three tips for getting alignment:

Let structure follow strategy: The organizational structure should facilitate, not inhibit, the strategy implementation effort. Structure should support strategy, not vice versa.

Encourage systems alignment through budgets and incentives: Use budgets to manage and control funds and emphasize investments that support the strategy. Tying incentives to key initiatives is a powerful technique for achieving alignment.

Understand that your culture counts: The organization's culture influences the employees to respond in specific ways when faced with challenges. Members of a performance-based culture will quickly synchronize efforts and find ways to support any new strategic initiative.

"Every system is perfectly designed to produce the results you are getting. If you want different results you probably have to change the system."

☐ Let functions work separately

☑ Work across functions

Specialization by function is necessary for effective general management. The major functions typically include:

- Marketing and sales—Creates demand
- Engineering/R&D—Provides product leadership
- Operations—Delivers goods and services to match demand
- Human resources—Attracts and retains the right people
- Finance—Funds the business and provides control

The functional managers must understand the corporate and business strategies, estimate the resources and capabilities required for their accomplishment, and then compare these requirements with current capacities. Functional managers should also set functional goals, which should be specific and within their control.

The challenge that all firms face is to coordinate the activities of functional units to achieve common goals and keep them from operating as independent or competing "silos." A culture of collaboration and shared values facilitates such coordination.

Functional strategies should be developed to describe how each functional area will support the business strategy. There should be a logical linkage from the needs of customers to business strategies to effective functional strategies and strategic alignment across the functions.

The derivation of functional strategies produces a list of issues that must be addressed in order for the functional areas to meet their goals. These issues then must be translated into specific, manageable actions. Action plans should include:

- Milestones (interim goals)
- Budgets
- Timetables
- Assigned responsibilities

In summary, these action plans define who is going to do what, by when, within specified budgets.

To integrate the action plans, group the functional plans by topic. When more than one function must work on a topic, they must plan their efforts jointly to avoid redundancies and conflicts. If problems surface, top managers must intervene and provide leadership to create the necessary cooperation.

Here are three things to remember as you work to achieve cross-functional integration:

Ensure that the functional managers understand how the strategic initiatives support the strategies: The implementation of any new strategic initiative will require some adjustment in the functional areas. If functional managers and their employees fail to consider the big picture, the result will be inadequate or conflicting support.

Use cross-functional teams to implement new strategic initiatives: With a skilled leader, these teams can be a source of efficiency and creativity. The teams must have the authority to make any necessary changes.

Reduce conflict by rotating managers through different functional areas: Zeal for one's specialty and the natural tendency to seek efficiency for one's home function can cause conflict on cross-functional teams. Having team members with experience in various functional areas will enhance cooperation and contribute to the development of the next generation of general managers.

"The functional units must work in concert to produce the desired results."

☐ ~~Wait for results~~ to happen

☑ Execute with discipline

Carefully crafted strategic initiatives and plans are of little value until they are executed successfully. Effective execution requires the right people to do the right things consistently.

A good multi-year history of solid performance consists of multiple individual years of successful results. The same holds true for failure: most firms that fail do so gradually, rather than in one catastrophic moment. Discipline and dedication are required to ensure successful strategy implementation and sound performance.

A firm's leaders must model the traits of discipline and dedication. Leaders establish standards for the employees and set the true tone for the culture, regardless of what is posted on the wall or written in the annual report. Thus, discipline and dedication should be attributes of the right people.

Your human resources function should reinforce disciplined action and dedication through its systems of evaluation, rewards, and promotion. Many firms find that individual progress reports are useful tools in reinforcing discipline. These reports might simply ask each employee what he or she did during the current period (often one or two weeks) and what is planned for the next period.

Planning and budgeting reports are more formalized and often quantitative progress reports at the group level. They should be produced at frequent and consistent intervals and their results should be communicated to the appropriate managers. Workers should be aware of the state of the organization, so they can be part of the solution when problems arise and take pride in their efforts when goals are achieved.

Project management is also an important technique for implementing strategic initiatives with the discipline to stay on budget and meet schedules. It is essential to break complex projects into manageable action steps that identify a critical path and to track progress against the plan.

Here are three tips that will help you with executing your strategy:

Act consistently and consistently act: Execution is about attention to detail, budgets, and deadlines. Mistakes will be made and compromises will be required. Deliberate and sustained effort will ultimately ensure the best chances for your strategy.

Link the organizational reward system and strategy execution: The reward system of a firm focuses on and influences both individual and group behaviors. Good execution depends on a reward system that signals what is desired. Highly motivated employees will drastically improve the chances of successful execution.

Foster an open and supportive organizational culture: The individuals involved in executing a new strategy must feel free to question supporting activities. Both successes and failures need to be understood so that requisite new skills and systems can be developed to support the strategic initiatives being implemented or so that the initiatives may be revised to allow successful implementation.

"History has belonged to those who execute best; strategies can be readily copied."

☐ ~~Trust the initiative to work~~

☑ **Monitor and improve**

The results of a business should be monitored to determine if strategic initiatives are being implemented on schedule and within budgeted resources. A firm's environment and competitive situation should also be monitored to ensure that strategies and initiatives remain logical and to identify emerging or pressing opportunities and threats.

To execute strategies, employees must maintain control of the activities that are their responsibilities. Rapid feedback regarding results is a powerful motivator to fully assume responsibility, achieve goals, and improve performance. An associated challenge, though, is setting up data-collection systems that are accurate and cost-effective in providing the necessary feedback.

The best data-collection systems capture performance at the time it occurs, use effective coding systems to describe the events of interest, and label the performance data for efficient analysis. Those who are managing the strategy implementation effort need the data in reasonable time so they can react appropriately. Data should be collected both internally from operations and externally from customers and the industry.

A review of current data allows employees to compare actual performance against their standards or goals. This comparison should reveal deviations from or exceptions to plans and, if substantial, prompt investigations.

A review of data accumulated over time enables managers to detect trends and extrapolate future results. Historic data are particularly valuable for leading indicators, such as incoming sales orders and backlogs, which are likely predictors of future demand. Trends in the economy and competitive environment are similarly useful.

If the data indicate problems, managers should strive to understand the underlying causes and correct them or adapt to them as quickly as possible. When data signify strong performance, managers should also aim to understand causes and to praise and reward those responsible to reinforce their positive behaviors and attitudes.

Here are three ideas to help you monitor, evaluate, and react:

Monitor for success, not control: The purpose of monitoring is to minimize the effects of poor performance and maximize the benefits of good performance. The key to achieving these goals is to provide feedback so employees can anticipate problems and opportunities and better perform their jobs.

Keep your eye on the strategic prize: Don't let the monitoring and evaluation efforts focus attention on short-term setbacks to the neglect of the essential strategy implementation effort. A good control system should encourage adaptability and creativity rather than punish shortcomings or require inflexible commitment to predetermined milestones.

Monitor selectively: You can't monitor everything, so select metrics that both matter and give early warning of variations from plans and assumptions. What you monitor signals what you consider to be important, so choose metrics wisely. Be open to new information; emergent trends can be as important as deliberate plans.

"You can't manage what you don't measure."

☐ Stay the course

☑Learn, change, and institutionalize

Our global business environment is constantly changing at a rapid pace. To survive, businesses must learn and change. No ultimate strategic weapon lasts long in business. Strategies are readily copied and even patents eventually expire.

Planning and implementing strategies provide opportunities for institutional learning. Such learning requires posing probing questions that challenge the status quo and seek new information. In order to formulate new strategies, you must evaluate and question your past experiences and current practices, as well as investigate industry and societal trends. The continuous cycle of planning, implementing, and evaluating strategies leads to learning and subsequent change.

The perpetual process laid out in these 24 steps describes one general approach to this cycle. You should adapt it to your firm, institutionalize it, and constantly improve it through learning. The value of learning is that knowledge builds on itself. Continuous learning is thus the foundation of continuous improvement.

The ways of learning include experience, observation, research, scanning, and monitoring. The sources of insight include your own operations and employees, customers, suppliers, competitors, and society.

With the appropriate structure, systems, and culture in place, the transfer of learning will take place routinely within your business. This transfer will drive much of the change in your organization as you do things differently because you have learned what must be done and how to do it better. Change occurs most readily in a culture of intellectual curiosity and discipline, one with an emphasis on experimenting as well as producing results.

Leaders must take an active role in managing change in their organizations. Large-scale change can take years and requires patience without concession. Day-to-day change also requires a consistent effort. It bears repeating that leaders set the true tone for the culture and standards for employees. If they do not model change individually and collectively, no one will change.

Here are three suggestions to help you institutionalize learning:

Recognize that a learning culture is an organization's key to the future: Insights into markets generate important understanding of strategic opportunities. A learning culture that fosters curiosity will improve your chances of discovering the next big opportunity.

Understand and accept that learning is about change: Build a sense of urgency for learning by openly discussing the risks of not changing. Create time for learning, reflecting, sharing information, and building trust.

Make learning one of your competitive advantages: Institutionalize debate, allow criticism, and tolerate failure. Learn to face reality through unbiased lenses—or a competitor will force you to do so.

The 24 steps that we have discussed provide a framework for planning and executing strategy. The process, though, is a never-ending cycle. Constantly changing environments, customers, competitors, and employees require strategic management to be an ongoing process, institutionalized within the organization, executed with discipline, and built on learning.

"Produce and compete or perish."
—Thomas Timings Holme

"After a business implements a strategy, competitors will react, and the firm's strategy will need to adapt to meet the new challenges. There is no stopping point and no final battle. The competitive cycle continues on perpetually. Produce and compete or perish."

—Thomas Timings Holme

"Before devising strategies, you must understand the competitive landscape as it exists and as it is changing."

"Strategy is a long-term concept and, most importantly, deals with change."

The McGraw-Hill Mighty Manager's Handbooks

The Powell Principles
by Oren Harari (0-07-144490-4)

Details two dozen mission- and people-based leadership skills that have guided Colin Powell through his nearly half-century of service to the United States.

Provides a straight-to-the-point guide that any leader in any arena can follow for unmitigated success.

How Buffett Does It
by James Pardoe (0-07-144912-4)

Expands on 24 primary ideas Warren Buffett has followed from day one.

Reveals Buffett's stubborn adherence to the time-honored fundamentals of value investing.

The Lombardi Rules
by Vince Lombardi, Jr. (0-07-144489-0)

Presents more than two dozen of the tenets and guidelines Lombardi used to drive him and those around him to unprecedented levels of success.

Packed with proven insights and techniques that are especially valuable in today's turbulent business world.

The Welch Way

by Jeffrey A. Krames (0-07-142953-0)

Draws on the career of Jack Welch to explain how workers can follow his proven model.

Shows how to reach new heights in today's wide-open, idea-driven workplace.

The Ghosn Factor

by Miguel Rivas-Micoud (0-07-148595-3)

Examines the life, works, and words of Carlos Ghosn, CEO of *Nissan* and *Renault*.

Provides 24 succinct lessons that managers can immediately apply.

How to Motivate Every Employee

by Anne Bruce (0-07-146330-5)

Provides strategies for infusing your employees with a passion for the work they do.

Packed with techniques, tips, and suggestions that are proven to motivate in all industries and environments.

The New Manager's Handbook

by Morey Stettner (0-07-146332-1)

Gives tips for teaming with your employees to achieve extraordinary goals.

Outlines field-proven techniques to succeed and win the respect of both your employees and your supervisors.

The Sales Success Handbook

by Linda Richardson (0-07-146331-3)

Shows how to sell customers—not by what you tell them, but by how well you listen to what they have to say.

Explains how to persuasively position the value you bring to meet the customer's business needs.

How to Manage Performance

by Robert Bacal (0-07-148439-8)

Provides goal-focused, common-sense techniques to stimulate employee productivity in any environment.

Details how to align employee goals and set performance incentives.

Managing in Times of Change

by Michael D. Maginn (0-07-148436-1)

Helps you to understand and explain the benefits of change, while flourishing within the new environment.

Provides straight talk and actionable advice for teams, managers, and individuals.

The Handbook for Leaders

by John H. Zenger and Joseph Folkman (0-07-148438-8)

Identifies 24 competencies essential for becoming an effective and extraordinary leader.

Provides a systematic program for attaining, developing, and implementing the skills.

About the Authors

Wallace Stettinius is Visiting Lecturer in Business Administration at the University of Virginia's Darden Graduate School of Business and Senior Executive Fellow at Virginia Commonwealth University. He teaches MBA and executive education courses in management, corporate governance, and executive development, and has served as director of a number of publicly and privately held corporations as well as chairman and CEO of a NASDAQ company.

D. Robley Wood, Jr., DBA, is Professor and Coordinator of the Strategic Management Area within the Department of Management at Virginia Commonwealth University. He has been engaged in teaching, research, and consulting related to all aspects of strategic management for over 30 years. His research has appeared in such publications as the *Strategic Management Journal*, *Academy of Management Journal*, and *Long Range Planning*.

Jacqueline L. Doyle, PhD, is Visiting Assistant Professor of Business Administration and former General Motors Post Doctoral Fellow at the Darden School, where she teaches MBA and executive education courses in corporate strategy and operations management. She has consulted with a variety of U.S. businesses in the areas of strategy and productivity improvement.

John L. Colley, Jr., DBA, is the Almand R. Coleman Professor of Business Administration at the Darden School, where he teaches courses in corporate strategy, corporate governance, and general management. He has served as chief of operations for the Hughes Aircraft Company and as a director for numerous corporations.

While this is their first collaboration, other titles from these authors include *Case Studies in Service Operations, Corporate and Divisional Planning, Corporate Governance, What Is Corporate Governance?* (with George W. Logan), and *Corporate Strategy* (with Robert D. Hardie).